GRANDPARENTING

Loving Our Children's Children

9 STUDIES FOR INDIVIDUALS OR GROUPS

LifeGuide®
BIBLE STUDIES

PHYLLIS J. LE PEAU
AND ANDREW T. LE PEAU

David + Linda,
When are we going to meet
again at the lake?! Such
a good memory.
Blessings as you grandparent.
Phyllis
Andy

IVP Connect

An imprint of InterVarsity Press
Downers Grove, Illinois

InterVarsity Press
P.O. Box 1400, Downers Grove, IL 60515-1426
ivpress.com
email@ivpress.com

InterVarsity Press® is the book-publishing division of InterVarsity Christian Fellowship/USA®, a movement of students and faculty active on campus at hundreds of universities, colleges, and schools of nursing in the United States of America, and a member movement of the International Fellowship of Evangelical Students. For information about local and regional activities, visit intervarsity.org.

LifeGuide® is a registered trademark of InterVarsity Christian Fellowship.

All Scripture quotations, unless otherwise indicated, are taken from THE HOLY BIBLE, NEW INTERNATIONAL VERSION®, NIV® Copyright © 1973, 1978, 1984, 2011 by Biblica, Inc.™ Used by permission. All rights reserved worldwide.

While any stories in this book are true, some names and identifying information may have been changed to protect the privacy of individuals.

Cover image: © Jodie Griggs / Getty Images

ISBN 978-0-8308-3111-1 (print)
ISBN 978-0-8308-6320-4 (digital)

Printed in the United States of America ♾

 As a member of the Green Press Initiative, InterVarsity Press is committed to protecting the environment and to the responsible use of natural resources. To learn more, visit greenpressinitiative.org.

P 25 24 23 22 21 20 19 18 17 16 15 14 13 12 11 10 9 8 7 6 5 4 3 2 1

Y 38 37 36 35 34 33 32 31 30 29 28 27 26 25 24 23 22 21 20 19 18 17

Contents

Getting the Most Out of *Grandparenting*

One of the delights of our life is to slip into the room where one or more of our grandchildren are asleep, look at them, pray for them, and kiss them good night. Just to be with them in their waking hours is pure joy (most of the time). And to see them grow, develop, and learn is like reliving the thrill of seeing our children grow, develop, and learn.

It has been said that grandchildren are the reward for not killing your kids. That might be a bit of an overstatement, but grandchildren are certainly a gift. A wonderful gift from God that merits great care and stewardship. The longing of our hearts is to grandparent well the thirteen we've been blessed with—so far! (It's an important part of a grandparent's job description to always hope for more.)

How delighted we are to play games with them, read to them, take them on outings, make meals for them, teach them new skills, and more! We try to spend as much time with them as we can, and that never seems to be enough, at least to us. Because grandparents are free from the same responsibilities as parents, we have a certain freedom in our relationship with grandchildren. We can love them completely free from the same expectations or demands that are rightly part of a parent's role. We can thus offer acceptance, confidence, and security that can build a foundation for the character of the children throughout their lives. As we love them we can help instill a deep sense of God's love for them and the importance of their relationship with him.

Although this is a guide for grandparents, we don't just concern ourselves with the grandchildren. We often include the parents in the application and discussion. Our relationships with our adult children have a profound influence on our relationship with our grandchildren.

One of the core prerequisites for grandparenting well is to maintain strong and healthy relationships with our adult children who are now parents. This is a great gift we can give to our grandkids—a healthy, loving relationship with their parents.

This can be difficult at times. We may have a history of hurts and dysfunctional patterns to overcome. In addition, when one of our children marries, the spouse brings a whole new family culture into the mix, which can present its own challenges.

We used to ask ourselves how to parent well; now we ask how we grandparent well. To get answers we ask advice from those who have been grandparents longer than we have. We pray and ask the Lord for guidance. We take time to discuss and reason things through. And, of course, we look to Scripture for help and guidance. That is what this guide can help you with. Gathering to study as a group of grandparents can make available the wisdom of those who have had more or different experiences.

As is often noted, there are very few examples of healthy and functional families in the Bible. Often what we learn from stories in the Bible is what *not* to do. But of course these negative examples can be helpful to us as we think about our grandparenting.

Many grandparents, of course, have taken on the role of parenting because, for a number of possible reasons, the parents themselves are not able to do so. These grandparents are heroes who deserve our respect and support. As a consequence, though, some of what is found in this guide may not be applicable to such situations. Their relationships with their sons-in-law or daughters-in-law may be limited or nonexistent. They also may not have the luxury of being able to step aside and allow the next generation to take the lead.

Something else to keep in mind is that different cultures see the role of grandparents and elders differently. We come from a Western context, and that informs our perspective. That is not necessarily a better context or perspective than others, so we want those from other settings who use this guide to adapt it as appropriate so they may be encouraged in their grandparenting.

One of the features of LifeGuide Bible Studies is the "Now or Later" section at the end of each study. We encourage you to take these seriously. In them we give some practical steps for growing relationships with our children and grandchildren. Not every suggestion will be appropriate, needed, or useful for every grandparent. So pick those that can help you nurture, repair, or build relationships in your family.

In this guide we will look at the importance of blessing our grandchildren, the place of prayer in the lives of grandparents, what it is to tell the next generation about God's goodness, the essential goal to love those who marry into our families, the consequences of favoritism, the fact that it is never too late to change, and finally to consider when it is time to step aside.

Most Bible study guides are meant to lead a person or a group through the passage or topic in forty-five to sixty minutes. Because of the depth and significance of our role as grandparents and the value of the input from each other in a group, you may want to consider extending your time for each study. This could be done in one of three ways. One is to simply make each meeting an hour and a half or two hours. Another is to devote two meetings to each study. The final option is for each person to do the Bible study on their own before each meeting. This could make the Bible study more efficient and give more time to share ideas, wisdom, and practical suggestions.

Paul said his aim was to "present everyone fully mature in Christ" (Colossians 1:28). That's what grandparenting is about also. Paul sought to build up others "with all the energy Christ so powerfully works in [us]" (Colossians 1:29). So can we, as we love our children's children.

Suggestions for Individual Study

1. As you begin each study, pray that God will speak to you through his Word.

2. Read the introduction to the study and respond to the personal reflection question or exercise. This is designed to help you focus on God and on the theme of the study.

3. Each study deals with a particular passage so that you can delve into the author's meaning in that context. Read and reread the passage to be studied. The questions are written using the language of the New International Version, so you may wish to use that version of the Bible. The New Revised Standard Version is also recommended.

4. This is an inductive Bible study, designed to help you discover for yourself what Scripture is saying. The study includes three types of questions. *Observation* questions ask about the basic facts: who, what, when, where, and how. *Interpretation* questions delve into the meaning of the passage. *Application* questions help you discover the implications of the text for growing in Christ. These three keys unlock the treasures of Scripture.

Write your answers to the questions in the spaces provided or in a personal journal. Writing can bring clarity and deeper understanding of yourself and of God's Word.

5. It might be good to have a Bible dictionary handy. Use it to look up any unfamiliar words, names, or places.

6. Use the prayer suggestion to guide you in thanking God for what you have learned and to pray about the applications that have come to mind.

7. You may want to go on to the suggestion under "Now or Later," or you may want to use that idea for your next study.

Suggestions for Members of a Group Study

1. Come to the study prepared. Follow the suggestions for individual study mentioned above. You will find that careful preparation will greatly enrich your time spent in group discussion.

2. Be willing to participate in the discussion. The leader of your group will not be lecturing. Instead, he or she will be encouraging the members of the group to discuss what they have learned. The leader will be asking the questions that are found in this guide.

3. Stick to the topic being discussed. Your answers should be based on the verses that are the focus of the discussion and not on outside authorities such as commentaries or speakers. These studies focus on a particular passage of Scripture. Only rarely should you refer to other portions of the Bible. This allows for everyone to participate in in-depth study on equal ground.

4. Be sensitive to the other members of the group. Listen attentively when they describe what they have learned. You may be surprised by their insights! Each question assumes a variety of answers. Many questions do not have "right" answers, particularly questions that aim at meaning or application. Instead the questions push us to explore the passage more thoroughly.

When possible, link what you say to the comments of others. Also, be affirming whenever you can. This will encourage some of the more hesitant members of the group to participate.

5. Be careful not to dominate the discussion. We are sometimes so eager to express our thoughts that we leave too little opportunity for others to respond. By all means participate! But allow others to also.

6. Expect God to teach you through the passage being discussed and through the other members of the group. Pray that you will have an enjoyable and profitable time together, but also that as a result of the study you will find ways that you can take action individually and/or as a group.

7. Remember that anything said in the group is considered confidential and should not be discussed outside the group unless specific permission is given to do so.

8. If you are the group leader, you will find additional suggestions at the back of the guide.

1

A Grandfather's Blessing

Genesis 48:1-20

We had taken care of our three granddaughters for five days while their parents went on a well-deserved vacation. Now the parents had returned and we all sat around the table. The two of us talked about each child, one by one, what we liked and appreciated about each one, the great things they had done while their parents were gone, how well they had behaved, how much we loved them, and how grateful we were that each was our grandchild.

As we talked about them, our granddaughters beamed. They were receiving our blessing.

We bless our grandchildren when we show them affection with touch and hugs. We bless them by spending time with them doing the things they love—books, sports, projects, play. We bless them when we pray for them. We bless them when we tell them God values them and is at work in them.

The world of our grandchildren will be full of challenges, difficulties, disappointments. Grandparents can offer a foundation of blessing that will be a safe harbor for them when life is stormy.

GROUP DISCUSSION. Name one thing you enjoy about being a grandparent. (Yes, for now, just one!)

PERSONAL REFLECTION. Has grandparenting turned out to be similar to or different from what you expected?

Genesis 37–47 tells the story of Jacob (later called Israel) and his twelve sons. The older ones were jealous of Joseph and sold him into slavery. But in Egypt Joseph became a powerful leader, second only to Pharaoh, who organized the country's food production to deal with the coming famine. This led to Jacob and his sons being reunited with Joseph when they came to Egypt to buy food. Now at the end of his life, Israel blesses Joseph's sons who were born to him while he lived in Egypt. *Read Genesis 48:1-20.*

1. Imagine you had been present when Jacob delivered his blessing. How would you picture the scene, including the feelings and atmosphere of the occasion?

2. Describe the relationship between Joseph and his father.

3. How would you describe your relationship with your adult children?

4. How would you characterize Jacob's relationship with God and why (especially see vv. 3-7, 11, 15-16)?

5. While Israel's prayer in Genesis 48:15-16 is one of blessing the two boys, why do you think it is introduced with, "Then he blessed Joseph and said . . ."?

6. How have you or might you bless your adult children?

7. What do you see of the past, the present, and the future in Israel's blessing (vv. 15-16, 19-20)?

8. How do you think the faithfulness of God to Israel affected his blessing of his son and grandsons?

9. Israel kisses and embraces the boys in verse 10, and in verse 14 he puts a hand on their heads. What role does touch play in blessing our grandchildren or children?

10. How can Israel's blessing of his grandchildren be a model for you?

11. What are other ways you have blessed your grandchildren?

12. How do you think your grandchildren have been or would be affected by receiving your blessing?

Ask the Holy Spirit to reveal to each grandchild how blessed they are by God. Pray for opportunities for you to bless them. Pray that you will see and take advantage of the opportunities he gives.

Now or Later

In their book *The Gift of the Blessing*, Gary Smalley and John Trent write that there are five elements to a blessing: meaningful touch, spoken words (and written words), expressing high value, picturing a special future, and an active commitment to the one blessed.

With these elements and Israel's blessing of his grandchildren in mind, write a blessing for each of your grandchildren. If possible, read it aloud to each of them and then give them a written copy. This can be done in a family gathering or when each child is dedicated to the Lord or baptized. If it is not possible to do it in person, you could send it to them.

In your blessing tell the grandchild (or child) how much you love them, what you like about them, what you see of God's work in them now and in their future, how you pray for them, and your commitment to their future. You might include the meaning of their name and tie it to a passage of or theme in Scripture. You could also give them some meaningful object along with it to remind them of the blessing—like a cross, a bookmark, a picture of Jesus with children, or something that is relevant to their name.

2

Praying for Our Grandchildren

Ephesians 1:15-22; 3:14-21

Phyllis often tells this story: "My grandmother died without seeing her prayers answered. For years she had prayed that her children would come to know Jesus. On her deathbed she begged my mother to tell her that she would see her again in heaven. But my mom was too honest of a woman and knew that she would not. She could not comfort her mother with those words. In fact, none of my grandmother's six children could. Although each of them adored her, they rejected the Lord she adored.

"Some years later my parents were beginning to make plans for their divorce. My mother calmly wrote to my grandfather to ask if she could come home with us girls. Immediately my grandfather sent the letter to my Uncle Frank (my mom's brother) who by this time was a follower of Jesus. My uncle immediately drove to my parents' place and once again told them the good news about Jesus. As a result, my mom and dad became Christians. Not only were they reconciled to God and to each other, my home was saved. As a result of their prayers and nurture, my sisters and I are walking with Jesus today.

"My spiritual journey was not only profoundly influenced by my parents but by my grandmother, who prayed fervently for them."

GROUP DISCUSSION. What motivates you to pray?

PERSONAL REFLECTION. Who has prayed for your spiritual welfare? How do you think you have been affected by this?

In Ephesians 1:3-14 Paul bursts out with an effusive statement on the amazing wealth of spiritual blessing we have in Christ Jesus. This is the foundation of his prayer that we find in the next verses. The way he prays can be a model of how we can pray for our grandchildren. *Read Ephesians 1:15-22.*

1. What characterizes Paul's prayer life as seen in verse 16-17?

2. How would you describe the when, where, and what of your prayer life?

3. What specifically did Paul pray for the Ephesians (vv. 17-19)?

4. What difference could answers to any one of these requests make in the lives of your grandchildren?

---

5. Paul then gets carried away describing the power of the God he prays to. What does he say about that power (vv. 19-22)?

---

6. *Read Ephesians 3:14-21.* Paul interrupts his letter with a second prayer for the Ephesians. Why is it significant in the prayer that he says, "every family in heaven and on earth derives its name" from the Father (vv. 14-15)?

---

7. In Ephesians 3:14, Paul mentions kneeling in prayer. But sometimes in the Bible people stand, sit, or lie prone in prayer. What difference to you, if any, does your posture in prayer make and why?

8. What requests does Paul make for the Ephesians in this prayer (vv. 16-19)?

_____

9. Which request strikes you as something you would especially like to pray for your grandchildren and why?

_____

10. What does it mean "to know this love [of Christ described in v. 18] that surpasses knowledge—that you may be filled to the measure of all the fullness of God" (v. 19)?

_____

11. Look again at the description of God in 1:19-20 and 3:20. How are your prayers for your children and grandchildren affected by praying to such a God?

12. What encouragement, direction, help, or motivation do Paul's prayers give you to pray faithfully for your children and grandchildren?

Pray for your grandchildren. Ask the Lord that each one might both know Jesus better and the hope that they have in him. Pray for any grandchildren who do not yet know Jesus that they will come into a personal relationship with him.

Now or Later

• Pray one of the two prayers of Paul for each grandchild. As you pray, put their name in the place of those who Paul was praying for. For example, "For this reason, because I know about ____'s faith in the Lord Jesus Christ and his [her] love for all God's people, I give thanks for him [her] . . ." and so forth through Ephesians 1:15-22.

• Write to each child and tell them what you have prayed for them. If the children are too young to understand, write to their parents.

3

From Generation to Generation

Psalm 78:1-8

We were concerned when our first child was born. Our children would be the fourth generation of Christians. In situations like that, faith can merely be part of a family's surroundings and culture that doesn't sink in at a personal, conscious level. It's just background music. As people grow and change, they often leave their parents' values behind. Faith could seem unnecessary or optional. Sometimes people even come to think of it as harmful. It happens in many strong Christian families. Would it happen in ours?

A few years ago one of our sisters gave us a collage that featured pictures of our family from four generations. She typed across the bottom, "Great is thy faithfulness to all generations." Though there are no guarantees about how anyone turns out, we can rely on God's faithfulness.

GROUP DISCUSSION. Take a minute to reflect on your spiritual journey. What part did parents or grandparents play or not play in that journey?

PERSONAL REFLECTION. What would you like to say to your parents or grandparents about their influence in your spiritual

life? Put it down in the form of a letter and consider sending it
to them if they are still alive.

In this passage we will consider how the psalmist passed on the
faithfulness of God and his commands to the next generations,
even as it had been passed on to him. *Read Psalm 78:1-8.*

1. How does the psalmist express the urgency of passing on to
the next generation what he has been taught (vv. 1-4)?

2. What specifically does the psalmist want to pass on (vv. 2-5)?

3. What truth from Scripture or what stories of God's faithfulness in your life have you passed on or could you pass on to
your grandchildren?

4. The psalmist says he wants to pass on both history and commands. Why are either insufficient by themselves while both are necessary together?

5. Verse 5 mentions that God "commanded our ancestors to teach their children" his word. This was a task not only for parents and grandparents but for the whole nation of Israel. In addition to direct instruction, what are other ways families and churches can engage in effectively passing on the biblical attitudes and values to the next generation?

6. What three goals for teaching the next generation are mentioned in verse 7?

7. How do you respond to these goals as you think about passing on to your grandchildren God's truth and your history with him?

8. What are the negative consequences the psalmist wants to avoid (v. 8)?

9. What signs do you see of the next generation being faithful and not being faithful to God?

10. In the remaining sixty-four verses of this psalm the writer goes on to recount the specifics of Israel's history from Moses to David. He notes their failures as well as their faithfulness. What stories could you pass on from successes and failures in your life that might help your grandchildren to avoid the same mistakes?

11. It is impossible to speak of all the years of God's faithfulness in one sitting. What ideas have you tried or might you try to regularly invest in your grandchildren's spiritual lives?

12. What barriers do you face in trying to pass on who God is and what he has done?

Thank God for his great faithfulness to you and to your children and your children's children. Pray that the Holy Spirit writes on your heart the deep desire for you to pass on God's commands and truth to your grandchildren so that "they would put their trust in God and would not forget his deeds but would keep his commands." Ask God to help you overcome the barriers that might be keeping you from investing spiritually in your grandchildren.

Now or Later

Think about and thank God for the specific times that he has been faithful in your life. Talk to God about your failures to follow him as well as your faithfulness to him. Look for opportunities to share these stories as well as Scripture as you teach your grandchildren about God.

4

Nurturing Contentment

1 Timothy 6:2-10

When our oldest son, Stephen, was about ten years old, he said, "You know, I wish I were an only child." Since he had three younger siblings, we wondered if there had been some major conflict among them that we hadn't noticed.

"Why do you say that?" we asked. "Don't you like your brothers and sister?"

"Oh, they're fine," Stephen replied. "But if I were an only child, then I could have all the stuff to myself."

"Well, not actually, Stephen. Just because you would be an only child wouldn't mean we would give you everything you wanted or asked for. It wouldn't be good for you to be spoiled like that. We are responsible to help build your character."

He thought for a minute and then said, "You know, I guess you're right. It's not the kids that are the problem—it's the parents!"

As grandparents we also have the opportunity to help nurture character and spiritual maturity. Especially in a world that entices us constantly with more and better, this can be a challenging endeavor.

GROUP DISCUSSION. How did you try to make sure your children didn't get spoiled with material things when you were raising them?

PERSONAL REFLECTION. What is my attitude toward money? Is it a cause of worry? Do I see it as a tool to achieve my goals? When do I think I have enough? How do I honor God with it?

Paul has given much instruction throughout his first letter to Timothy about what to believe and how to conduct the corporate life of the church. In 1 Timothy 3:15 he says he is changing topics, now offering instructions on how people are to conduct themselves personally in God's household. We will be looking at one aspect of that teaching. *Read 1 Timothy 6:2-10* (beginning with the last sentence of verse 2).

---

1. Look at Paul's description of those who do not agree with godly teaching (vv. 4-5). In your own words, how would you describe such people?

---

2. Perhaps surprisingly, Paul ends this rather sharp description by mentioning people "who think that godliness is a means to financial gain." What is the connection between this and the rest of the description he has just given in verses 4-5?

---

3. What contrasting description does Paul then offer in verses 6-8?

4. How are godliness and contentment connected?

---

5. On a scale from 1 to 10 (1 being very discontent and 10 being very content), how would you rate the level of contentment in your family? Explain.

---

6. What practical, everyday differences would it make in our lives if we were more content?

---

7. How can godly contentment counteract the divisiveness Paul emphasizes in verses 4-5?

---

8. Many children in the Western world are growing up in a wealthy culture where great emphasis is placed on what we own. Society pushes us to continually get more, have the latest experience, and get excitement from something new. What might we do to encourage our grandchildren to be content with what they have?

9. In verse 9 Paul mentions how the rich can fall into temptation and trouble. How can money lead to these results?

10. What stories could you tell your grandchildren that could warn them about such an approach to life?

11. It often has been pointed out that Paul doesn't say, "Money is the root of all evil," but rather, "The love of money is a root of all kinds of evil" (v. 10). How can we tell how much we love money?

12. In light of this passage, how would you say that your patterns of giving things to your grandchildren do or do not contribute to their contentment? Explain.

Here is a sample of what you might bring to God in prayer: "Lord, the greatest desire of our hearts is that our grandchildren love you, follow you, and live godly lives. We have just discussed the destructive effects of loving money and wanting to get rich. We have seen that godliness with contentment is great gain. Help us to live a life of contentment because of all that we have in you and thus model and nurture godliness and contentment in our grandchildren."

Now or Later

- Spend more time in Scripture looking at the importance of contentment and its role in your life as a growing Christian. Read and meditate on such passages as Psalm 131, Proverbs 19:23, Ecclesiastes 4:8, Luke 3:14, Philippians 4:10-14, and Hebrews 13:5-6.

- Intentionally talk with your grandchildren about the destructiveness of living to "get more," what contentment is, and how it is related to godliness.

- Grandparents love to give to their grandchildren. Make a list of some other ways you can give to them without buying stuff, and make plans to work your way through the list in the coming months.

5

Loving Your In-Laws

When your children marry, their spouses can be like sons and daughters. But relationships with the spouses of your children can also be fraught with tension and difficulties. Each time one of your children marries it is like adding not just a new member but a whole new culture to your family. To work hard and sacrifice to maintain good connections with them not only shows wisdom and maturity but can have a major influence on your relationship with your grandchildren. One of the best ways to love your grandchildren is to love their parents unconditionally.

GROUP DISCUSSION. What has helped you to grow as a parent-in-law?

PERSONAL REFLECTION. What has it been like for you to add adult children to your family?

In this study we will consider what Naomi's relationship with Ruth can teach about loving and accepting your in-laws as if they were your own children. The story takes place in the time of the judges in Israel, which falls between the time of Joshua and that of King Saul. *Read Ruth 1:1-18.*

1. Naomi has lost her husband and two sons in the country of Moab. How would you describe the relationship she has with her daughters-in-law?

_____

2. What reasons does Naomi give for them to return to their mother's home rather than go with her (vv. 11-13)?

_____

3. What are specific ways that you have cared for the spouses of your children?

_____

4. What strikes you about Ruth's response to Naomi (vv. 16-17)?

_____

5. What do these words tell you about the kind of mother-in-law Naomi must have been?

6. The book of Ruth emphasizes that Ruth was from Moab, repeating this seven times (Ruth 1:4, 22; 2:2, 6, 21; 4:5, 10). How would ethnic differences affect a relationship between a mother-in-law and a daughter-in-law?

7. What has helped build your relationship with the spouses of your children?

What has made it difficult?

8. Upon their return to Judah, Ruth went to the fields to pick up leftover grain (as was customarily permitted for the poor) so that she and Naomi could eat. As it turned out she worked in the field owned by Boaz, who was related to Naomi's husband. *Read Ruth 2:8-13.* What was Boaz's response to Ruth working in his field and why (vv. 8-13)?

9. Because of Ruth's strong relationship with Naomi, now Boaz was positively disposed toward Ruth. In what ways have you seen good relationships between in-laws have positive ripple effects in other relationships?

---

10. In the story Ruth is identified as Naomi's daughter-in-law. But Naomi consistently addressed her as "daughter" (Ruth 1:11-13; 2:2, 22; 3:1, 16, 18). Why is your relationship with the spouses of your children important?

---

11. Ruth continued to be well treated by Boaz, so Naomi gave Ruth specific instructions on how to build her relationship with Boaz. Boaz responded positively to Ruth's overtures and agreed to pursue marriage with her. *Read Ruth 4:13-17.* Describe the Lord's blessing to Boaz, Ruth, and Naomi at the end of this story.

---

12. What blessings have come to your family through the spouses of your children?

Thank God for your children and their spouses. Ask the Lord to show you ways you can love and communicate favor to them. Talk to him about the next steps for you to take to make this happen.

Now or Later

- Sometimes relationships with your children and their spouses can be strained. There may have been angry words, hurt feelings, disappointments, and even harmful actions. We can't force change on other people. We can only do what is right ourselves. Journal about anything you have done in your relationship with your kids or their spouses that you need to ask forgiveness for. Consider before God if there are any changes in behavior you need to make to build or nurture a good relationship with them. In severe situations involving, for example, addiction, we may need to change our behavior to tough love. Consider getting help from a counselor to understand how to do this.

- Write a letter to each spouse of your children. Tell them what you love and appreciate about them. Tell them why you are grateful for them and why you are glad to have them in your family.

6

The Problem
with Favoritism

Genesis 27:30-41; 37:1-36

"I don't know how Gabe has turned out to be the man that he
is," Aunt Neat said. She had tears in her eyes, thinking about
her younger brother. When my (Phyllis's) young grandmother
knew she was dying she asked her sister, Barlow, to care for her
young sons Gabe and Harrison. Barlow agreed.

When the time came for Barlow to take over, everyone knew
who her favorite was. In the dead of winter she sent Harrison
out with warm coat, hat, scarf, mittens. Gabe wore a light jacket
that flapped open. The supply of candy that Barlow gave to
Harrison was huge. Gabe had none. When Harrison and dad
visited Barlow as adults, she greeted Harrison enthusiastically
and for all practical purposes ignored Gabe.

As I listened to Aunt Neat, I too looked at Gabe, my dad,
and thanked God for the man he turned out to be in spite of
being an orphan, uneducated, and raised under the dark cloud
of blatant favoritism.

GROUP DISCUSSION. When have you felt that you were someone's favorite or clearly not the favorite?

PERSONAL REFLECTION. What pain have you experienced from
feeling your parents or grandparents did not love you as much

as others? Or how did your parents or grandparents demonstrate unconditional love to everyone?

After Abraham's son Isaac married Rebekah, she became pregnant with twin boys—Esau the first born and Jacob. From the beginning Isaac loved Esau more, while Rebekah loved Jacob (Genesis 25:24-28). One of the ways this favoritism was demonstrated was when Rebekah and Jacob deceived Isaac into giving his blessing to Jacob, the younger son, instead of Esau who, as the oldest, was suppose to receive it (Genesis 27:1-29). *Read Genesis 27:30-41.*

1. Here we see how Esau responded when he found out what had happened. What effect did Rebekah's favoritism and deception have on her husband, Isaac?

2. What emotional reactions did Esau have when he found out?

3. What damage have you seen in families caused by favoritism?

4. Jacob fled his home to escape Esau's retribution and went to be with his Uncle Laban. He married Laban's daughters Leah and Rachel (Genesis 29:1-30). Leah gave Jacob several children, but only much later did Jacob's beloved Rachel give birth to Joseph and Benjamin. *Read Genesis 37:1-36.* How has the pattern of favoritism that began with Isaac and Rebekah continued in the next generation (vv. 3-4)?

5. How did Jacob show favoritism to Joseph?

6. In the rest of Genesis 37 what were the results of Jacob's partiality toward Joseph?

7. While we may aim to treat everyone equally, it is not unusual for us to be drawn to some people more than others. That can happen with children and grandchildren too, even when we love them all equally. Do you agree or disagree with that? Explain.

8. How can you or do you work to make sure you show the same love to all?

---

9. Often, we think of the damage of favoritism done to the "un-favored." How was Joseph's own character damaged by being the favorite (see especially vv. 2, 5-10)?

---

10. How have you seen favored children affected negatively in such ways?

---

11. All around us there are multigenerational patterns like favoritism. Joseph, however, broke the family dysfunction. Instead of taking revenge on his brothers, he said, "'You intended to harm me, but God intended it for good.'... And he reassured them and spoke kindly to them" (Genesis 50:19-21). What hope does this story and work of God give you?

12. What are ways that you can make sure that you are not showing partiality to your children or grandchildren?

Sit quietly before the Lord. Ask him to reveal to you ways you need to grow in how you love and accept each child and grandchild. Ask the Lord specific ways you can love them better. Thank him for each grandchild by name.

Now or Later

- Reflect on each child and grandchild. Are there any that you feel you have not loved well? Ask God for forgiveness. Think about a first step to take to make that right. Ask the person for forgiveness. Do something special that expresses love to them. Ask for wisdom and help from other grandparents.

- If you identified one or more grandchildren you might have neglected, after a game or performance your grandchild participated in, write a note of affirmation for the improvement you saw, a show of good sportsmanship, what you enjoyed, or the like.

- Sometimes we can be blind to the favoritism we show others. One practical step could be to ask someone we know and trust for perspective on how we treat our family members. Doing so can be risky, and we can be tempted to become defensive. So we would need to ask God for an open spirit.

- How much do you rely on gift giving to communicate love to your grandchildren? Consider whether this might be over-indulging them with material things. How can you also give them other more valuable and lasting gifts by helping to build into them character traits such as honesty, joy, resilience, stick-to-itiveness and the ability to delay gratification?

7

Family Forgiveness

Matthew 18:21-35

No one spoke of it but the grandchildren knew. Their father and uncle, Jack and Timothy, were not on speaking terms. They were distantly polite and civil at family gatherings, but they ignored each other as much as possible. They had had a disagreement about a joint financial venture and stopped talking to each other. Their parents grieved over the rupture. The children in both families knew something was wrong but couldn't verbalize it. They didn't see as much of each other as before and wished things could be "like they were before."

Jack and Timothy's parents knew they had said all they could say to their sons and that to bring it up more would just make the rift grow bigger. But they prayed. On it went for years. Then, seemingly out of nowhere, Timothy asked Jack to forgive him for his part of the fracture. Jack was surprised but said he would. Not much else changed for a while. But after much soul searching, Jack went to Timothy and asked the same. Slowly trust was rebuilt until yes, miraculously, things went back to "like they were before."

GROUP DISCUSSION. How does it feel when you approach someone to ask for forgiveness?

PERSONAL REFLECTION. What does it mean to you to be forgiven?

In this study we will look at Jesus' mandate to forgive and to consider how this forgiveness affects our children and grandchildren. *Read Matthew 18:21-35.*

1. Peter asks Jesus how many times he needed to forgive his brother or sister who sins against him. How do you think Peter responded to Jesus telling him to forgive not seven times but seventy-seven times?

2. Jesus tells a parable to extend his teaching on forgiveness. In this story who do the master, the first servant, and the second servant each represent?

3. Compare and contrast the two servants.

4. What point is Jesus making with the two debts and the two debtors?

5. Why are injuries in families often some of the most difficult to forgive?

_____

6. What are the results of the first servant not forgiving?

_____

7. What can result from refusing to forgive in a family?

_____

8. As seen in this passage, how seriously does God take it when we don't forgive others?

_____

9. Is there anyone in your family who you need to forgive or to ask forgiveness of? What is the first step you could take to reconcile with that person?

If no one came to mind, it may be that you've already built a pattern or culture of forgiveness in your family. If so, how was that accomplished?

10. Describe how your grandchildren could or do thrive in an environment in which forgiveness is lived out freely.

11. Sometimes relationships can be broken for very serious reasons. In such cases, forgiving doesn't mean we should go back into an abusive relationship. In that kind of situation, what does forgiveness involve?

12. What do Jesus' opening words "The kingdom of heaven is like" tell you about the implications of his teaching on forgiveness?

Pray that the Holy Spirit will reveal to you where you need to extend forgiveness and where you need to ask for forgiveness. Ask him for the wisdom, strength, and courage to do what needs to be done. Pray that the Lord would equip you to provide an environment in which forgiveness is lived out freely. Thank the Lord for relationships with kids and grandkids that are grounded in love and forgiveness.

Now or Later

List strengths and weaknesses in relationships in your extended family. Consider what consequences there may have been from lack of forgiveness between family members. Place these issues before God in prayer as well as the possibility of finding a professional counselor for serious issues.

8

Never Too Late to Change

2 Chronicles 33:1-20

Uncle Frank was an alcoholic who came home drunk every night. The family had given up on him. One evening as he walked home with uncertain steps, swaying because of the alcohol in his body, the Holy Spirit came upon him. He knelt, almost falling to his knees, drunk. Miraculously he gave his life to Jesus and stood up sober. The impossible happened. For the rest of his life Uncle Frank served Jesus as a pastor and a youth camp director. He wanted kids to meet Jesus and avoid the misery of his first thirty-five years.

GROUP DISCUSSION. Why does change seem to be more difficult the older we get?

PERSONAL REFLECTION. What are the painful relationships in your life where you think change is impossible?

In this study we will look at the miraculous change that God brought about in King Manasseh. *Read 2 Chronicles 33:1-20.*

1. In spite of the godliness of his father, King Hezekiah, Manasseh did great evil. Describe each evil and why it was detestable "in the eyes of the LORD" (vv. 1-6).

2. What promise did God make to the tribes of Israel (vv. 7-8)?

3. What promises has the Lord given Christians that can encourage us as grandparents?

4. In verse 10 we read, "The LORD spoke to Manasseh and his people, but they paid no attention." What are ways that God speaks to us?

5. Why is it hard to listen well to God sometimes?

6. Describe a situation when you heard God well or were slow to hear the voice of the Lord regarding your relationships with your children or grandchildren.

---

7. What happened as a result of the king and the people not listening to God (v. 11)?

---

8. Then Manasseh changed (vv. 12-13). What does the phrase "humbled himself" before the Lord communicate?

---

9. How can we benefit from having an accurate picture of who we are and who God is?

---

10. Manasseh suffered the consequences God clearly said would come from disobedience—exile from the land. How can God sometimes use natural consequences to bring about change in people?

---

11. What evidence of change do we see in Manasseh's life (vv. 14-20)?

---

12. What changes would you like to see in yourself regarding your children or grandchildren?

Bring to God the changes you'd like to see in your life. Ask for wisdom on what steps you should take to facilitate change in you. Thank him that because of his power, change can happen even in our hearts as we humble ourselves before the Lord.

Now or Later

Read passages of Scripture where God brought about miraculous change in peoples' lives. For example, Saul of Taurus (Acts 9:1-22), Simon Peter (Mark 14:66-72; Acts 2:14-41), the Ethiopian eunuch (Acts 8:26-40), the man blind from birth (John 9:1-34), the two disciples on the road to Emmaus (Luke 24:13-35). In some of these stories there is instant change, and in others the change is gradual. Let these be an encouragement to you as you consider the possibility of change.

9

When It Is Time to Step Aside

2 Samuel 19:31-40

Our daughter and her family came to live with us temporarily. Because we thought it was important to clearly communicate our different roles, we said to the grandkids, "When your mom and dad are here, they are the first boss, and we are the second boss. But when mom and dad are gone, then we are the first boss." The grandchildren seemed to understand the order of things. However, when they wanted an extra cookie, they came to the second boss.

This is just one small way we need to step aside and allow the next generation to take the leadership role. Our role changes from one of leading to one of supporting and encouraging.

GROUP DISCUSSION. When you started having children, how did your parents tend to "take over" with your children, even when you were present? How did you feel about this?

PERSONAL REFLECTION. As you reflect back on raising your children, what do you appreciate about your parents' involvement with them? What caused you difficulty?

The rebellion of Absalom against his father, King David, was over. Absalom had been killed in battle, and David grieved his death. But the king also wanted to honor Barzillai for his service to David during Absalom's rebellion (2 Samuel 17:27-29). In this passage we will see the wisdom and grace of Barzillai as he recognized it was time for him to step aside and turn over leadership and service for the king to a younger person. *Read 2 Samuel 19:31-40.*

1. What invitation does David give to Barzillai (vv. 31-33)?

2. How does Barzillai respond to David (vv. 34-37)?

3. What aspects of Barzillai's aging process are similar to your own?

4. How do you feel about your aging?

5. Barzillai thinks it is time for him to step aside from being counsel to the king. What has it been like for you to step aside as you see your children take more leadership in the family?

6. When is it time to reduce the amount of advice you give the next generation? Explain your thinking.

---

7. The king is blessing and showing honor to the elder. What are one or two specific ways that you have been blessed and honored by your children and grandchildren?

---

8. David showed deference to Barzillai by asking him to come to Jerusalem. How does he respond to Barzillai's request to return home instead (vv. 38-40)?

---

9. Based on his comments to David (vv. 34-37), what character traits do you see Barzillai?

---

10. Which of these traits of Barzillai would be helpful to nurture as you let go and move to the next stage?

11. A common source of tension between grandparents and their adult children is that they have different parenting styles. When have you experienced this tension either with your parents or your children as they parent?

---

12. How can you grow in letting go and giving your adult children more freedom and encouragement in their parenting?

Pray that the Lord will reveal to you when and how you should take the initiative to step aside from primary roles, as Barzillai did. Ask the Lord for wisdom, grace, and strength to grow in your ability to support and encourage your children and grandchildren in their lives.

Now or Later

Probably the time to step aside from our leadership in the family is sooner than we would think by instinct. We are so used to guiding and leading our children, it can be a hard pattern to change, to give the next generation the space they need to begin leading their own families and maybe the extended family as well.

Reflect on and write down ways that you would like to graciously step back as you watch your children lead their families. Then jot down specific ways that you want to support and encourage them in this adventure of child rearing.

Leader's Notes

Leading a Bible discussion can be an enjoyable and rewarding experience. But it can also be *scary*—especially if you've never done it before. If this is your feeling, you're in good company. When God asked Moses to lead the Israelites out of Egypt, he replied, "Please send someone else" (Exodus 4:13)! It was the same with Solomon, Jeremiah, and Timothy, but God helped these people in spite of their weaknesses, and he will help you as well.

You don't need to be an expert on the Bible or a trained teacher to lead a Bible discussion. The idea behind these inductive studies is that the leader guides group members to discover for themselves what the Bible has to say. This method of learning will allow group members to remember much more of what is said than a lecture would.

These studies are designed to be led easily. As a matter of fact, the flow of questions through the passage from observation to interpretation to application is so natural that you may feel that the studies lead themselves. This study guide is also flexible. You can use it with a variety of groups—student, professional, neighborhood, or church groups. Each study takes forty-five to sixty minutes in a group setting.

There are some important facts to know about group dynamics and encouraging discussion. The suggestions listed below should enable you to effectively and enjoyably fulfill your role as leader.

Preparing for the Study

1. Ask God to help you understand and apply the passage in your own life. Unless this happens, you will not be prepared to lead others. Pray too for the various members of the group. Ask God to open your hearts to the message of his Word and motivate you to action.

2. Read the introduction to the entire guide to get an overview of the entire book and the issues that will be explored.

3. As you begin each study, read and reread the assigned Bible passage to familiarize yourself with it.

4. This study guide is based on the New International Version of the Bible. It will help you and the group if you use this translation as the basis for your study and discussion.

5. Carefully work through each question in the study. Spend time in meditation and reflection as you consider how to respond.

6. Write your thoughts and responses in the space provided in the study guide. This will help you to express your understanding of the passage clearly.

7. It might help to have a Bible dictionary handy. Use it to look up any unfamiliar words, names, or places. (For additional help on how to study a passage, see chapter five of *How to Lead a LifeGuide Bible Study,* InterVarsity Press.)

8. Consider how you can apply the Scripture to your life. Remember that the group will follow your lead in responding to the studies. They will not go any deeper than you do.

9. Once you have finished your own study of the passage, familiarize yourself with the leader's notes for the study you are leading. These are designed to help you in several ways. First, they tell you the purpose the study guide author had in mind when writing the study. Take time to think through how the study questions work together to accomplish that purpose. Second, the notes provide you with additional background information or suggestions on group dynamics for various questions. This information can be useful when people have difficulty understanding or answering a question. Third, the leader's notes can alert you to potential problems you may encounter during the study.

10. If you wish to remind yourself of anything mentioned in the leader's notes, make a note to yourself below that question in the study.

Leading the Study

1. Begin the study on time. Open with prayer, asking God to help the group to understand and apply the passage.

2. Be sure that everyone in your group has a study guide. Encourage the group to prepare beforehand for each discussion by reading the introduction to the guide and by working through the questions in the study.

3. At the beginning of your first time together, explain that these studies are meant to be discussions, not lectures. Encourage the members of the group to participate. However, do not put pressure on those who may be hesitant to speak during the first few sessions. You may want to suggest the following guidelines to your group.

☐ Stick to the topic being discussed.

☐ Your responses should be based on the verses that are the focus of the discussion and not on outside authorities such as commentaries or speakers.

☐ These studies focus on a particular passage of Scripture. Only rarely should you refer to other portions of the Bible. This allows for everyone to participate in in-depth study on equal ground.

☐ Anything said in the group is considered confidential and will not be discussed outside the group unless specific permission is given to do so.

☐ We will listen attentively to each other and provide time for each person present to talk.

☐ We will pray for each other.

4. Have a group member read the introduction at the beginning of the discussion.

5. Every session begins with a group discussion question. The question or activity is meant to be used before the passage is read. The question introduces the theme of the study and encourages group members to begin to open up. Encourage as many members as possible to participate, and be ready to get the discussion going with your own response.

This section is designed to reveal where our thoughts or feelings need to be transformed by Scripture. That is why it is especially important not to read the passage before the discussion question is asked. The passage will tend to color the honest reactions people would otherwise give because they are, of course, supposed to think the way the Bible does.

You may want to supplement the group discussion question with an icebreaker to help people get comfortable. See the community section of *Small Group Idea Book* for more ideas.

You also might want to use the personal reflection question with your group. Either allow a time of silence for people to respond individually or discuss it together.

6. Have a group member (or members if the passage is long) read aloud the passage to be studied. Then give people several minutes to read the passage again silently so that they can take it all in.

7. Question 1 will generally be an overview question designed to briefly survey the passage. Encourage the group to look at the whole passage, but try to avoid getting sidetracked by questions or issues that will be addressed later in the study.

8. As you ask the questions, keep in mind that they are designed to be used just as they are written. You may simply read them aloud. Or you may prefer to express them in your own words.

There may be times when it is appropriate to deviate from the study guide. For example, a question may have already been answered. If so, move on to the next question. Or someone may raise an important question not covered in the guide. Take time to discuss it, but try to keep the group from going off on tangents.

9. Avoid answering your own questions. If necessary, repeat or rephrase them until they are clearly understood. Or point out something you read in the leader's notes to clarify the context or meaning. An eager group quickly becomes passive and silent if they think the leader will do most of the talking.

10. Don't be afraid of silence. People may need time to think about the question before formulating their answers.

11. Don't be content with just one answer. Ask, "What do the rest of you think?" or "Anything else?" until several people have given answers to the question.

12. Acknowledge all contributions. Try to be affirming whenever possible. Never reject an answer. If it is clearly off-base, ask,

"Which verse led you to that conclusion?" or again, "What do the rest of you think?"

13. Don't expect every answer to be addressed to you, even though this will probably happen at first. As group members become more at ease, they will begin to truly interact with each other. This is one sign of healthy discussion.

14. Don't be afraid of controversy. It can be very stimulating. If you don't resolve an issue completely, don't be frustrated. Move on and keep it in mind for later. A subsequent study may solve the problem.

15. Periodically summarize what the group has said about the passage. This helps to draw together the various ideas mentioned and gives continuity to the study. But don't preach.

16. At the end of the Bible discussion you may want to allow group members a time of quiet to work on an idea under "Now or Later." Then discuss what you experienced. Or you may want to encourage group members to work on these ideas between meetings. Give an opportunity during the session for people to talk about what they are learning.

17. Conclude your time together with conversational prayer, adapting the prayer suggestion at the end of the study to your group. Ask for God's help in following through on the commitments you've made.

18. End on time.

Many more suggestions and helps are found in *How to Lead a LifeGuide Bible Study*.

Components of Small Groups

A healthy small group should do more than study the Bible. There are four components to consider as you structure your time together.

Nurture. Small groups help us to grow in our knowledge and love of God. Bible study is the key to making this happen and is the foundation of your small group.

Community. Small groups are a great place to develop deep friendships with other Christians. Allow time for informal interaction before and after each study. Plan activities and games that will help you get to know each other. Spend time having fun together going on a picnic or cooking dinner together.

Worship and prayer. Your study will be enhanced by spending time praising God together in prayer or song. Pray for each other's needs and keep track of how God is answering prayer in your group. Ask God to help you to apply what you are learning in your study.

Outreach. Reaching out to others can be a practical way of applying what you are learning, and it will keep your group from becoming self-focused. Host a series of evangelistic discussions for your friends or neighbors. Clean up the yard of an elderly friend. Serve at a soup kitchen together, or spend a day working on a Habitat house.

Many more suggestions and helps in each of these areas are found in *Small Group Idea Book.* Information on building a small group can be found in *Small Group Leaders' Handbook* and *The Big Book on Small Groups* (both from InterVarsity Press). Reading through one of these books would be worth your time.

Before each study, you may want to put an asterisk by the key questions you think are most important to cover for your group, in case you don't have time to cover all the questions. As we suggested in "Getting the Most out of *Grandparenting*," if you want to make sure you have enough time to discuss all the questions, you have other options. For example, the group could decide to extend each meeting to ninety minutes or more. Alternatively, you could devote two sixty-minute sessions to each study.

Study 1. A Grandfather's Blessing. Genesis 48:1-20.
Purpose: To see the importance of blessing our grandchildren through word and prayer as well as physical touch.
Question 1. Joseph and his father were reunited after thinking they would never see each other again. And not only did Jacob get to be reunited with Joseph, but God allowed him to see Joseph's sons. Now Jacob is on his death bed and soon will once again say goodbye to Joseph. But before his death God allows him to tenderly bless his grandsons. The love and grace and presence of God is deeply felt.

Since Joseph's sons were born before the seven years of famine (Genesis 41:50) and Jacob had been in Egypt for seventeen years (Genesis 45:11; 47:28), Manasseh and Ephraim would probably be in their early twenties. Though question 1 is not meant to focus on Jacob's inheritance to his sons, here is some information in case questions come up. Jacob had twelve sons. Here Jacob adopts Joseph's two sons as his own (Genesis 48:5), possibly to honor the memory of his beloved wife Rachel (Genesis 48:7) by giving her son Joseph a double portion of the inheritance. This had implications when the nation went back to the Promised Land under Moses four hundred years later. Since the tribe of Levi was not given an equal share of land (Leviticus 25:32-34), that left shares for eleven tribes. But since Joseph's sons each got a portion of the land, that brought the division of land back to twelve.

Question 2. Jacob and his other sons lived in Goshen (Genesis 45:10), where they could have pastureland for their flocks. Joseph continued to be busy near the center of government. So a visit to Goshen would be a special occasion (Genesis 48:1-2).

Joseph and Jacob share mutual respect and love for each other. They share mutual respect and love for God. They are full of gratitude for having been reunited and that Jacob is allowed to see Joseph's sons. In verse 12 Joseph "bowed down with his face to the ground." There are only two more places in Genesis where someone bowed down before another human. (In Genesis 19:1 Lot bows down to the angels who he saw as guests, and in 33:3 Jacob bows down seven times before his older brother, Esau.) This was a sign of honor to an elder or a respected guest.

Question 3. This can be a difficult question to manage because our relationships with our adult children are not always positive. Allow time for honest responses, but try to guide the time in such a way that not only one or two people get to talk. To get the ball rolling and to set an example of honesty, be ready to share from your experience, especially if no one begins to talk after a few moments.

Question 6. Allow participants time to think. These questions concern one of the most important applications of this passage. Not only are we blessing our grandchildren but we bless their parents by giving them the emotional and spiritual confidence and assurance that is vital in raising children. Making the effort to bless our children can be life changing for the children and the grandchildren. While we probably won't bless our grandchildren by telling their futures, as Jacob did, we can deeply affect their futures by our love, affirmations, and prayers.

In case someone asks why Jacob asks who the boys are in verse 8 when he already mentioned them in verse 5, there are two possible reasons. One may be his bad eyesight, and the other is that it may be part of the ceremony of the blessing, as at baptisms when ministers will ask formally who is to be baptized, though they already know the answer.

In verse 12, since the two sons were young adults, "from Israel's knees" probably does not mean they were sitting "on his knees" but were likely kneeling before the aged Israel, either at his knees or between his knees.

Question 9. Though this question is not meant to focus on it, someone may ask why Jacob placed his hands opposite to where Joseph wanted them placed. As seen in verses 13-14, Joseph expects and tries to arrange things so that the older son (Manasseh) will receive the primary (right hand) blessing. But despite Joseph's protests in verses 17-18, Israel switches the order. (Note that already in verse 5 Israel listed the younger son first.) While the custom of giving preference to the oldest son was strong and well established in the ancient Near East, we frequently see this reversed in Genesis—Abel over Cain, Isaac over Ishmael, and Joseph getting a double portion over Reuben, the eldest of the twelve sons (see comments at question 1). Most significantly in this context, however, Israel received the primary blessing over his older brother, Esau. Though Israel received that blessing through duplicity, that is not the case here. Throughout Genesis God reverses human expectations, putting the first last and the last first.

Questions 10-11. This is a great time for grandparents to share ideas of how they have or would like to bless their grandkids. Such things as hugs, words of affirmation both in private and public, special outings with them, praying with and for them, loving and honoring their parents, telling them about Jesus and God's work in their personal lives, and so forth.

In your blessing, tell the grandchild how much you love them, what you like about them, what you see of God's work in them now and in their future, how you pray for them, and your commitment to their future. And of course give them hugs.

Study 2. Praying for Our Grandchildren. Ephesians 1:15-22; 3:14-21.

Purpose: To be motivated to pray regularly and fervently for our grandchildren, and to use the prayers of Paul in Ephesians as a model of what we can pray for them.

Question 1. "I have not stopped giving thanks for you" (v. 16). "Remembering you in my prayers" (v. 17). "I keep asking . . . God" (v. 17).

Question 2. To help set an open and accepting atmosphere, be ready to model openness and vulnerability by sharing your own prayer life, its strengths as well as its weaknesses. The point is not to have a contest of spiritual one-upsmanship but to encourage one another in prayer.

Questions 3. Verses 17-19 are the substance of his petitions, that they may have a Spirit of wisdom, may know God better, may have the eyes of their hearts opened to see their hope and the rich inheritance of God's people.

Question 4. Allow time for participants to reflect on the requests Paul made. Answers from God to Paul's requests could be life changing. Here is an opportunity for the group to imagine the specific, concrete effects that wisdom or knowing God better could have in the lives of their grandchildren.

Question 5. The power of God gives us great hope that our prayers can be answered.

Question 6. Paul is using a bit of word play here since the Greek words for "father" (*patera*) and "family" (*patria*) sound alike. But we don't have to know Greek to understand Paul's sentiment that God is the creator (the Father) of families. Families are his idea. They are founded by him and in him. In addition, the Christian community is often called the family of God. He extends his prayer to all in the family of God.

So when we pray for the welfare of our families and all who are in them, we know we are clearly praying within God's will, within the framework of his good plan for humanity. We can take great hope and comfort in that, even when our family situations may be troubled.

Question 7. Sitting (Exodus 17:10-13; 2 Samuel 7:18; 1 Kings 19:4), standing (2 Chronicles 20:5-13; 1 Samuel 1:26; 1 Kings 8:22; Job 30:20; Mark 11:25), kneeling (1 Kings 19:18; 2 Chronicles 6:13; Ezra 9:5; Daniel 6:10), and lying down or bowing with one's face to the ground (2 Samuel 12:16; 2 Chronicles 20:18; Ezekiel 11:13; Mark 14:35) are all postures of prayer in the Bible.

Those in your group may have very different feelings about or experiences of kneeling to pray. But hopefully the question will be at least a suggestion that there is a place for kneeling, and it could make a difference in our attitude to God.

Question 8. Take a moment to consider each request. These include being strengthened with God's power, having Christ dwell in our hearts, being rooted in love, having the power to grasp Christ's love for us, and being filled with the fullness of God.

Question 10. Allow the group to think through and attempt to discover for themselves what this passage means first before sharing from this note. If you or they need help, here are some thoughts from New Testament scholar Francis Foulkes.

The definite goal to which the Christian life must move, and for which therefore the apostle prays, is for his readers *to know the love of Christ*, to know how he loved and loves, and to experience his love in loving him and loving others for his sake. Yet even here Paul cannot escape the paradox. In the Greek between the verb and its object there is this qualification that apparently contradicts the verb—the love *surpasses knowledge* (cf. Phil. 4:7). The love of Christ is infinitely greater than anyone can fully know or imagine, and it is also much more than any object of knowledge; it is superior to knowledge (1 Cor. 8:1), even to spiritual knowledge (1 Cor. 13:2). It must find expression in experience, in sorrows and joys, trials and sufferings, in ways too deep for the human mind to fathom, or for human language to express.

The climax of the apostle's prayer for his fellow-Christians is that they *may be filled with all the fullness of God*. He thus prays ultimately that they may receive not any attribute of God, or any gift of his, not love, not knowledge, not strength, alone or in combination—but no less than the very highest he can pray for, the full indwelling of God. This "defies even the beginnings of our understanding" (Stott), but we should not miss the point of what the apostle is striving to express. Of course the eternal God can never be limited to the capacity of any one, or all, of his sinful creatures; at the same time Paul does not want to pray for anything less than that God's people may be filled to (*eis*) the very fullest of himself that he seeks to bring into their lives (see on 1:23). For his own life, and for those to whom he ministers, Paul wants no less than the Spirit's full indwelling (5:18). Of his fullness, and not just of a part of his nature, all may receive (John 1:16); and the goal for the individual and for the body must be nothing short of "the measure of the stature of the fullness of Christ" (4:13). (Francis Foulkes, *Ephesians* [Downers Grove, IL: InterVarsity Press, 1989, 2008], 112)

Study 3. From Generation to Generation. Psalm 78:1-8.
Purpose: To consider passing on and be motivated to pass on to future generations what past generations have taught us about God's faithfulness and commands so that the next generations, even children yet to be born, would know them, obey them, and put their trust in God.

While the group will only discuss the first eight verses of Psalm 78, it would be good for you as the leader to read and be familiar with the whole psalm beforehand. Some of the discussion will touch on topics raised in the rest of the psalm.

Question 1. Lead the group to unpack the content of this question. Help them sit with the verses and feel the emotion and commitment. This is the basis for motivating participants to pass on to their children and grandchildren God's commands, laws, and faithfulness.

The invitation of verse 1 seems to be urgent and heartfelt. What he is inviting them to participate in can make a difference for generations to come. People are to listen, pay attention, and do what he asks for the sake of their children's and grandchildren's relationship with and attitude toward God.

He states clearly what he is going to do. He doesn't waver. There are two "I will" and two "we will" statements in these four verses. He knows not only what he wants to do and say, but how he will do this. By moving from "I" to "we" he reinforces the idea that his message is to pass their heritage from one generation to the next.

Question 3. Allow time for silence for participants to think. Possibly allow more time for sharing than normal. This is an opportunity to learn about the life stories of those in the group as well as to get ideas for the kinds of things we might pass on to our grandchildren. The focus of this question is on God's faithfulness.

Question 4. Stories fill our imaginations, touching our emotions, the way precepts alone cannot. They tell us in a way that reaches our hearts both how to live and why to live. Someone once said that philosophically he wasn't sure what good and evil were, but reading *The Lord of the Rings* convinced him they were very real. That is why Jesus told parables and didn't merely list commands. Rules alone can turn us into legalists. But we also need clear instruction from the law and commands of God, which are the foundation of our lives and stories. They are to be known and obeyed.

Question 5. The psalmist likely has in mind instructions such as those found in Deuteronomy 4:9, 6:4-7, and 11:19.

In addition to straight education, think about other ways that values (good or bad) are passed on. How is our attitude toward money and possessions passed on? What about attitudes toward government or hospitality or media? Often these are not communicated by direct teaching, but they are communicated clearly nonetheless. How does that happen? And what might that tell us about effective ways to pass on biblical values to our children?

Question 6. Verse 7 is the core message of the passage and the ultimate goal for telling the next generation "the praiseworthy deeds of the LORD, his power and the wonders he has done."

Question 7. It might be good to thoughtfully list them again. Do group members find these goals encouraging or discouraging, realistic or unrealistic? Another way to ask the question is, How are you affected as you think about having a part in your grandchild's putting their trust in God, or not forgetting God's deeds?

Question 8. In the rest of Psalm 78 we read about the times the people of Israel forgot the wonderful things God did on their behalf from the days of Moses to David. A half dozen times the psalmist mentions the people forgetting God's goodness (Psalm 78:9-11, 17-22, 32, 36-37, 40-42, 56-58). In between those comments the psalmist mentions what God did to help them as well as how he judged them when they rebelled. One of the main points of the psalm is to help future generations avoid the judgment that can come from forgetting or ignoring God.

Question 9. The discussion could go one of two directions—what the group sees in society generally or what they see in their grandchildren in particular. Either is fine. Some members may not see or want to share any negative things about their grandchildren. Of course people should not be encouraged to share anything they don't want to. On the other hand, there could be help for them in the group. It could be a good time to remind the group of confidentiality. What is said in the group stays in the group.

Question 10. The focus of question 3 was on God's faithfulness. The focus here is on stories of our own successes and failures that might be of value to our grandchildren.

Question 11. You might need to be ready with some ideas to get the ball rolling.

- reading or telling stories from the Bible at nap time, bedtime, or whenever they enjoy being read to
- singing songs about Jesus with them or to them
- praying with them

- sharing answers to prayer
- speaking biblical truth when appropriate (love, sin, forgiveness, grace), but not use the Bible as a weapon against them
- verbally giving God credit for such things as creation, the seasons, their mom and dad, and so forth
- telling them stories from your life where you have seen God work or stories from the lives of their parents

Study 4. Nurturing Contentment. 1 Timothy 6:2-10.
Purpose: To consider how contentment is a vital part of godliness, and to be challenged to nurture our grandchildren in contentment, especially considering the value that our culture places on money and possessions.

Question 1. Lead the group in careful consideration of these characteristics. They are important as we discuss contentment, which is one of the topics Paul covers as he writes to Timothy about what he should teach. To avoid these attitudes and characteristics is part of the motivation for living a godly life of contentment. This is the kind of life we want our grandkids to experience.

Question 2. It could seem like the issue of money as a motivation comes out of nowhere. But Paul apparently sees some connection between money and the divisiveness he describes in verses 4-5. Give the group time to try to work this out. If they don't come up with something satisfactory, just move on. You could say, "Well, let's keep going and see if the rest of the passage gives us any clues." We think it will.

Question 4. Allow the group time to think and to put together the connection of godliness with contentment. As always don't just give them the answers.

To be content means I am grateful to God for who I am and what he has given me. It means I trust God to meet my needs for such essentials as food and clothing. It means I am focusing on God and others rather than getting more wealth. It means I am free to care for others and to give away to those in the world who are in need because God is caring for me. If I am not content, I may find myself jealous of or at odds with others.

Question 5. Often we want to present our families as perfect, so honest responses to this question may be slow in coming if they come at all. If this seems to be the case, remind participants that we are here as a community to love and care for each other, and they are safe to be vulnerable.

Question 8. No matter how much money we have, we can always think we aren't rich because we can think of others who have more. Yet most everyone in Western countries is wealthy compared to the rest of world. Part of our problem (and our sin) is not thinking about all those who have less—so much less.

The process of helping our children to be content with what they have begins inside us. The first step is to recognize how materially wealthy we are and acknowledge all that we have. The next is to develop a spirit of genuine gratitude to God for all that he has given us. All good things come from him. All that we have and are belong to him. When we acknowledge our wealth and have a heart of gratitude, we can model contentment to our grandchildren. So much of life is caught as well as taught.

Phyllis loves to tell the story first to our children, and now to our grandchildren, of her growing-up years when money was not in abundance in her home. "There were times when we actually had enough money only for oatmeal, which became our dinner. However, my dad always set aside tithes from whatever amount came in that week. Then on Sunday morning he got the tithes box down from the cabinet for us to take our portion to church. Tithing was impressed on me deeply, not from my dad's words but what he modeled before me."

When we model true contentment, we can teach kids about a heart of gratitude and remind them of specific things they have to be grateful for. We can offer prayers of gratitude regularly with them. We can help them to be aware of all the emotional and spiritual blessings they experience. We can teach them about needy kids in the world and suggest ways they can give to others. The list is endless. Be creative and be intentional.

Allow the group time to discuss and help each other in this important area of their grandkids' lives.

Question 12. Giving an abundance of gifts can be an easy pattern to fall into, but too much can lead to children placing too much value on material things. This leads to the kind of trouble in life that Paul describes in this passage. We have the wonderful opportunity to help nurture in our grandchildren deep contentment, and "godliness with contentment is great gain" (1 Timothy 6:6).

Note: At the end of the study, remind the group to read the book of Ruth. It is four short chapters and so will only take about ten minutes. While the group will not discuss the whole book, only selections, it will be helpful to have the whole story in mind, and there won't be time to read the whole book aloud at the next group meeting.

Study 5. Loving Your In-Laws. Ruth 1:1-18; 2:8-13; 4:13-17.

Purpose: To learn about loving and accepting our children's spouses.

Note: This study gives an overview of the book of Ruth by reading and discussing some selections while the material in between is summarized. Because of this you might find this discussion more challenging to lead. To help you lead this study effectively you need to read through the whole book at least twice, and even more if needed to become familiar and comfortable with the story. It would also be good to remind your group to read it before coming to the study.

Question 1. Help the group to not overlook the fact that Naomi is grieving over the loss of her husband and sons as you discuss the relationship she has with her daughters-in-law.

Question 2. One of the points of these questions is to emphasize Naomi's love for her daughters-in-law. She urged them to go back to their home because she thought it would be better for them. Their leaving her would have been another great loss to her, but Naomi wanted what was best for them rather than herself.

Question 3. Some in the group may have serious problems with the spouses of their children—addiction, unfaithfulness, abuse, and so forth. Be alert to this possibility. Not everyone has the kind of relationship Naomi had with Ruth. See "Now or Later" at the end of the study for more thoughts on this.

Question 4. Help the group not to slide over these familiar but powerful words. They are words of deep loyalty and love. Ruth is leaving her people, her culture, her town, all that is familiar to her, including her gods because of her love for and commitment to Naomi.

Question 5. What a wonderful mother-in-law Naomi must have been to elicit this love and loyalty from Ruth. She was like a mother to Ruth, and Ruth was like her daughter.

Question 6. Moabites descended from Lot's incestuous union with his daughter (Genesis 19:36-37) and lived east of the Dead Sea. Israel had had rocky relationships with Moab for hundreds of years (Numbers 25; Judges 3:12-17; 11:17). The differences between Israel and Moab were substantial and wide ranged—political, military, religious, cultural, and ethnic. These added layers of potential tension between Naomi and Ruth, and make their deep love and care for each other all the more remarkable.

Question 6 is phrased in a way that allows the group to discuss ethnic conflict as it might occur in the context of the book of Ruth or in the experience of group members. Both are legitimate aspects of the discussion and can be encouraged. There may be some group members who have in-laws of other ethnicities. This could be a source of delightful diversity or of tension—or both. Be sensitive to these possibilities while keeping in mind that God's clear intention in the book of Ruth was to show that he embraces (along with the line of David and of Jesus) different cultures and ethnic groups into his family.

Question 7. You will have to gauge the level of trust there is in your group. If some are not comfortable being open about issues they have, don't press too hard. Let group members know that no one will condemn or criticize each other for problems, and remind everyone as needed that what is said will be held in confidence in the group and not be shared with any others. You are all there to support one another. As a leader, you can set the tone by being honest about difficulties you may have with your children or their spouses.

You also need to be ready to not let the discussion get out of hand or full of complaining about the faults of the in-laws or about barriers the in-laws create. We are here to look at ourselves and how we can do what is right in those relationships. Sometimes there are simply limits in those relationships that cannot be completely surmounted. The question then is, in the context of that reality, how can I act in the most constructive way?

When our children divorce, relationships with former spouses can take on new and very challenging dimensions. If this is the situation for one or more of those in the group, give opportunity (without pressuring) for people to voice their questions and concerns. Don't be too quick to give answers, though. Sometimes people just need to be heard.

Question 8. Regarding Ruth 2, gleaning (picking up leftover grain from a field that had been harvested by the owner) was a systemic way Israelite society provided for the poor (Leviticus 19:9-10; 23:22). Not all landowners, however, followed Moses' law, and they chased off those who gleaned, perhaps violently. That is why both Naomi and Boaz mention concern about what might happen to Ruth in other fields.

Question 11. When Naomi hears about Boaz's kindness to Ruth she says, "The LORD bless him! He has not stopped showing his kindness to the living and the dead. That man is our close relative; he is one of our guardian redeemers" (Ruth 2:20).

When Naomi then gave Ruth specific instructions on how to build her relationship with Boaz, Ruth agreed to "do whatever you say" (Ruth 3:1-5). Boaz agreed to pursue marriage with her (Ruth 3:10-11). But first he had to settle with a relative more closely related to Naomi's husband, who had first choice to "redeem" Naomi's land. When the other relative found out it would also involve marrying Ruth, he refused, leaving the path clear for Boaz to do both (Ruth 3:12–4:12). Boaz thus became Ruth's husband.

Regarding Ruth 3–4, Boaz is acting as a "guardian-redeemer" (NIV) or what is known as a kinsman-redeemer. There really is no equivalent to this role in Western society. A kinsman-redeemer "was the nearest adult male blood relative who served as an advocate for any vulnerable and/or unfortunate clan member in order to correct any disruption to clan wholeness, well-being, or *shalom* (esp. through the redemption or restoration of property, persons, or lineage)." (K. Lawson Younger Jr., *Judges, Ruth,* NIV Application Commentary [Grand Rapids: Zondervan, 2002], 399.)

As you consider the many blessings that came to Naomi, Ruth, and Boaz, do not overlook the fact that Boaz and Ruth's son, Obed, was in the line of David—and so also in the line of Jesus.

Study 6. The Problem with Favoritism. Genesis 27:30-41; 37:1-36.

Purpose: To understand the negative effects of favoritism with children and to see how it affects not only the children but the grandchildren.

Note: If you think many in your group will not know the story well, you may need to spend a bit more time summarizing the narratives, which might mean you won't have time for questions 11-12. In any case, you, as the leader, will want to reread Genesis 25:19–50:26 beforehand so you have a good grasp of the storyline.

Questions 1-2. Sometimes our favoritism is deep but subtle, so we might be blind to it. Sometimes favoritism is overt and obvious. Either way favoritism can have negative ramifications, as we see here with Esau and Jacob, Isaac and Rebekah. Esau had a variety of emotional reactions—anger, bitterness, desperation, vengefulness.

The NIV includes a footnote to Genesis 27:36 that says, "*Jacob* means *he grasps the heel,* a Hebrew idiom for *he takes advantage of* or *he deceives.*"

Question 3. If the participants had siblings who were favored over themselves, it could be hard to share. Be comfortable with silence. Communicate gently that people don't have to say anything if they don't want to. As a leader, you can help set a tone of supportive openness for the group by being honest about your own experiences. So think ahead of time about what you might share.

Question 4. We see Jacob behaving like his father, Isaac, in that Jacob "loved" Joseph. Six of Jacob's sons and one daughter were from his wife Leah. Four sons were born from his wives' handmaids, while Joseph and Benjamin were from Rachel, Isaac's beloved wife. The passage says he loved Joseph because he was born to him in his old age. But it is safe to say it was also because he was born to his favorite wife, Rachel.

Actually the pattern of favoritism began with Isaac's parents. Abraham had two sons—Ishmael by his handmaid Hagar and Isaac by his wife Sarah. Though having a child by Hagar was Sarah's idea to ensure an heir, she grew to hate both Hagar and her son, and demanded they be banished (see Genesis 16:1-16; 21:1-20). So the dysfunctionality was found in three generations. Jacob imitated what he saw in his parents, and Isaac repeated what he saw in his parents.

Question 6. This question needs a close survey of Genesis 37. Lead them carefully through the passage to see all the evil results of favoritism: Joseph brings his father a bad report about his brothers (v. 2). The brothers hated him and could not speak a kind word to him (v. 4). "They hated him all the more" (v. 8). Joseph's brothers were jealous of him, and his father kept this in mind (v. 11). They plotted to kill Joseph (v. 18). Jacob expressed extreme grief and sorrow (vv. 31-35). Finally, Joseph ends up in Egypt, far away from home, family, and all that was familiar and precious to him (v. 36).

Question 7. We are naturally drawn to certain types of people and less to other types—whether they are relatives or not. Some of us are attracted to outgoing, lively people, others to those who are quiet and thoughtful. Others find creative, innovative people to be stimulating.

Such natural affinity is not the same as favoritism. And we can still love all equally. However, we are responsible to know ourselves and to be honest with ourselves about how we might have preferences and show that. Pretending or not being willing to admit such things is usually not constructive because the reality usually shows itself eventually. Better to face it so we can deal with it constructively than not tell ourselves the truth. So taking ownership of such feelings, even if they are mild, can lead to healthier relationships.

Question 9. In spite of Joseph knowing his brothers were jealous of him and even hated him, he freely told them about his two dreams that showed them bowing down to him. Joseph showed poor judgment in talking about his dreams in a way that caused further anger and resentment. While the dream revealed something true, Joseph didn't fully understand its implications or context. He didn't know he would be sold into slavery but as a result eventually save his whole family from famine. He didn't know the bowing down would be because the brothers didn't recognize him and thought he was someone else. Nor did he know that telling the dreams would be one of the causes for making the dream come true—one of the reasons they wanted to sell him into slavery. He was prideful. He did not admit his potential ignorance. Perhaps because his father loved him more than the others, he concluded that he must be very special indeed, causing him to think too highly of himself. This immaturity came back to bite him in more ways than one. It even made his father rebuke him.

Question 11. After Joseph was sold into slavery in Egypt, he eventually rose to power, becoming second only to Pharaoh, with the responsibility to oversee the nation's food production and storage so a famine could be avoided (Genesis 39–41). Because of the famine, his family came to Egypt for food, where, as the dream predicted, his brothers bowed down to him. They did not recognize him as their brother. But Joseph did not take vengeance on them. Instead he saved the whole family (Genesis 42–46). After their father died, however, the brothers feared Joseph would then take his revenge on them. Finally, Joseph completely broke the pattern of dysfunctionality that had plagued the family for generations. "Joseph said to them, 'Don't be afraid. Am I in the place of God? You intended to harm me, but God intended it for good to accomplish what is now being done, the saving of many lives. So then, don't be afraid. I will provide for you and your children.' And he reassured them and spoke kindly to them" (Genesis 50:19-21).

Joseph responded to his brothers personally and with a deep sense of God's purpose. He also recognized that God had been at work, redeeming evil deeds and turning them into good results. And how Joseph has changed! Once he was an arrogant teenager, but now he has a healthy, measured appreciation of his own importance, saying, "Am I in the place of God?" (Genesis 50:19).

Question 12. See "Now or Later" for a few practical suggestions.

Study 7. Family Forgiveness. Matthew 18:21-35.

Purpose: To look at Jesus' mandate to forgive, one of the most difficult yet essential practices in our lives, to consider the consequences of refusing to forgive, and to choose to grant forgiveness that is needed in relationship to our children and grandchildren.

Question 4. Jesus intentionally makes the contrast between the two debts ridiculous. One is so huge it could never be paid back. The other is quite small in comparison. We have been forgiven so much by God, how can we possibly not forgive others for the little ways they have offended us? Shouldn't we follow the example of our heavenly Father? After all, the offenses of others against me do not come near to how large my sin is toward God, who has provided me with everything I have and am.

Question 5. Many people and families are in extreme pain because of grudges or bitterness or lack of forgiveness in the family. As is often said, we can be hurt most by those who are closest to us. Family members know each other's points of vulnerability and can all too easily target those with harsh comments or hurtful actions.

Question 8. Be sure to consider the effects not only concerning the first servant but also concerning the second servant and the king.

Question 9. Forgiveness is not a sudden loss of memory. To forgive is not necessarily to forget. It also does not mean feelings of hurt are gone instantly. Sometimes when one decides to forgive, the memories of the pain or the feelings disappear. Instead, to forgive is a decision. It is a decision not to hold the injury that I have sustained over the head of the person who has hurt me, to in some way try to make them pay for what they did. It is the decision to release the power that we hold over another human being by withholding forgiveness from them.

It is a decision in which we need the help of the Holy Spirit to implement it. Each time a memory or a hurt feeling appears we can turn to the Holy Spirit and ask for the strength to not give in to the feeling or memory. It is committing our hurts and memories to him. It is asking him for his healing.

One of the motivations to forgive is to release from our souls the damage that comes from not forgiving, holding on to grudges and bitterness. That anger brings with it sickness to our souls.

As you prepare to lead this study think about the pain that could be elicited from participants because they are in situations where they have been hurt or have hurt others. Some situations could be very serious such as physical, sexual, verbal, or emotional abuse. We are called on to forgive, but we are not called to put ourselves or others back in harm's way. If these issues don't come up here, they could in response to question 11.

The second part of question 9 may provide a wonderful opportunity for participants to share ways they have built a culture of forgiveness in their families where it is commonplace and expected. People can be encouraged and given ideas to implement in their families. Be sure to pause between asking the two parts of question 9. Give people a chance to answer the first part before asking the second part about family cultures.

Question 11. See the comment above at question 9. As noted there, forgiveness doesn't necessarily mean a relationship of trust is fully restored. It means deciding not to hold the injury over the head of the person who has hurt me, to in some way try to make them pay for what they did. We are deciding not to extract some form of retribution. But if a person is still untrustworthy, it could be wise (not necessarily vengeful) to keep others away who might be harmed by that person.

Question 12. Jesus is saying "Forgiveness is a sign of the kingdom, and to forgive is kingdom living. I have brought the kingdom of God, and this is the only way of life in my kingdom. It is not an option to not forgive your brothers and sisters. This is serious enough that God will not forgive us if we do not forgive others."

Study 8. Never Too Late to Change. 2 Chronicles 33:1-20.
Purpose: To discover from the life of Manasseh that drastic change is possible.
Question 1. Don't just recite a list. Help the group describe what is involved in each one.

The high places (vv. 3, 17, 19) refers to pagan altars, which were often built on mountains or hilltops.

Baal (v. 3) means "lord" and refers to the Canaanite god who was a fertility god as well as a dying (fall) and rising (spring) deity. The plural, Baals, doesn't mean there were many such gods but that this one particular god had various sites and statues associated with it.

Asherah poles (vv. 3, 19) were possibly representations of trees since the goddess Asherah was associated with sacred groves. She was also the consort of the chief god in Canaanite and Amorite mythology.

The starry hosts (vv. 3, 5) refers to the sun, moon, planets, stars, and constellations that were closely associated with certain gods and humans, and which were thought to have influence on events on earth.

He sacrificed his children in the fire in the Valley of Ben Hinnom (v. 6) describes a practice that was strictly forbidden in the Pentateuch (Leviticus 18:21; Deuteronomy 18:10). The valley is just outside the southern walls of Jerusalem and was used as a garbage dump, where trash was continually burning, in Jesus' day.

Question 2. The promise referred to is found in such places as Exodus 15:17, Deuteronomy 28:1-7, 29:24-28, 31:19-20, and 2 Samuel 7:10.

Question 4. God speaks to us in many ways—through his Word, through prayer, through the advice and counsel of wise Christians, through the lessons learned by Christians of the past (history and tradition), through circumstances, through our own reasoning. Usually we hear God best when we blend these together rather than merely relying on one way.

Question 8. Pride is at the core of the fall of Adam and Eve as recorded in Genesis. It is at the core of each human being. Pride, maybe more than any other attitude or sin, breaks our relationship with God and with others. To humble ourselves before God or others is opposite to our nature and difficult to do. But to humble ourselves grants great reward. Humility doesn't mean we think of ourselves as worthless. It means we have an accurate picture of ourselves as God's creations and his stewards. We have come to terms with the fact that he is in charge and we are not.

Question 10. God is not the author of evil and suffering. In fact, he is the one trying to protect us from the suffering that comes from our disobedient actions. Think how much less suffering and distress there would be if people didn't steal, lie, commit adultery, or hurt others. The point of the question is not to ask why there is evil in the world if God is good. That would be too large to tackle in this study (and a bit off the subject). If that comes up, you may want to say, "That is a great question, and one that people have wrestled with for thousands of years. Unfortunately, we don't have time to cover that right now. However, we can discuss it later with anyone who wants to stick around after the study. Or we can schedule another time to talk about it." The point here is that some (not all) suffering is the consequence of our sin. And some suffering, as in this passage, is God-directed for a specific purpose that he wants to accomplish in us. That suffering, as for Manasseh, is so worth it if it means we bend to his will and honor God where we have refused to do so otherwise.

Study 9. When It Is Time to Step Aside. 2 Samuel 19:31-40.
Purpose: To consider the importance of stepping aside from our longtime role of leadership in the family, and to know when our role should become one of encouragement and support as our children lead their families.
Question 3. Barzillai acknowledges he is old. His senses of taste and hearing are affected. He saw himself as a potential burden to David. He knew that death was near.
Question 4. Growing old was not part of God's original plan when he created the world. Aging and death are the result of the fall in the Garden of Eden. The aging process is difficult for some and even more difficult for others. The fact that we are aging is sometimes hard to acknowledge. Lead this question with gentleness and with the goal that participants feel safe enough to give vulnerable responses.
Question 5. The loss of independence, sometimes a lost sense of purpose and of physical strength as we age, can make it difficult to let go of roles we've long held. Often our identity is wrongly placed on what we do. Sometimes pure denial that we are aging causes this difficulty. Sometimes it is simply not trusting the

next generation or refusing to allow them to learn from their mistakes as we had to. Sometimes it is just a long-standing habit. There are many reasons that make stepping aside difficult. Encourage the group to be open and honest in their responses.

Question 6. This question should lead to interesting discussion and probably differences of opinions. We think that it is good to give children freedom and encouragement to make decisions appropriate to each stage of life as they grow up. The decisions become bigger and more important as they mature. The goal is for them to become independent, responsible adults who make wise decisions. By the time they are young adults, it is usually best to wait until they ask for advice before giving it, and to make sure they want the advice when they ask. Certainly this is also true as they raise their own children.

Outside the Western world, elders typically continue to take a prominent role in the extended family, even as they age. If members of your group include, for example, those of Asian or African descent, there may be other perspectives on this question.

Question 7. There are countless ways that adult children "bless" and "honor" their parents, such as inviting them to be with and love their grandchildren, asking for advice or suggestions, overtly showing respect even as the parents age, praying for them, loving them with words and deeds, and so forth.

Question 8. Interestingly, the world of David was one that gave continuing honor and respect to the elderly, as do most cultures today outside the West. And so perhaps it is not surprising that David, though king, acquiesces to the wishes of his elder instead of pressing his own agenda for Barzillai to come to Jerusalem. Barzillai took the initiative to say that it was time for him to take a secondary role. He did not expect he should be in the forefront indefinitely. So, we need to likewise take the initiative in making such transitions.

Questions 9-10. Barzillai is a great model for "returning home" or letting go. You might need to ask questions within this question to help the group discover all the observations about him. For example: What was his state of mind as he returned home? What evidence is there that he was ready to and wanted to go home? What was his attitude to the past? To others taking his place?

As Barzillai returned, he was content. He acknowledged his age and limits, and was satisfied to go back home and live with these limits. He did not resent his old age. It seems that returning home was more important to him than being a part of the king's family. He was able to look at and connect with the past in a healthy way while not living in the past. He lived realistically and joyfully in the present. He did not try to prove himself, deny the changes in him or the changes in his new role. He did not seem to fear death. He received David's blessing and "returned home."

We do not know anything else for certain about Kimham except what is mentioned in this passage. Likely, though, he was a son of Barzillai. Right before David died, one of his charges to his son Solomon was to "show kindness to the sons of Barzillai of Gilead and let them be among those who eat at your table. They stood by me when I fled from your brother Absalom" (1 Kings 2:7).

Phyllis Le Peau worked with InterVarsity Christian Fellowship for over two decades in St. Louis and the Chicago metro area. She is also the author of several Bible study guides published by Zondervan and InterVarsity Press, including the LifeGuide Bible Studies Acts, Love, *and* Women of the New Testament. *She and her husband, Andy, have four married children and thirteen grandchildren.*

Andrew T. Le Peau is a writer and editor living in the Chicago area. He was the long-time associate publisher for editorial at InterVarsity Press where he worked from 1975 to 2016. Before that he was a campus staff member for Inter-Varsity Christian Fellowship, serving in the St. Louis area. He is the coauthor with Phyllis Le Peau of several Bible study guides, including James *and* Ephesians *in the LifeGuide Bible Study series, and author of* Heart. Soul. Mind. Strength. *(IVP) and* Mark Through Old Testament Eyes *(Kregel).*

What should we study next?

We have LifeGuides for . . .

LifeGuide®
BIBLE STUDIES

KNOWING JESUS
Advent of the Savior
Following Jesus
I Am
Abiding in Christ
Jesus' Final Week

KNOWING GOD
Listening to God
Meeting God
God's Comfort
God's Love
The 23rd Psalm
Miracles

GROWING IN THE SPIRIT
Meeting the Spirit
Fruit of the Spirit
Spiritual Gifts
Spiritual Warfare

**LOOKING AT
THE TRINITY**
Images of Christ
Images of God
Images of the Spirit

**DEVELOPING
DISCIPLINES**
Christian Disciplines
God's Word
Hospitality
The Lord's Prayer
Prayer

Praying the Psalms
Sabbath
Worship

**DEEPENING
YOUR DOCTRINE**
Angels
Apostles' Creed
Christian Beliefs
The Cross
End Times
Good & Evil
Heaven
The Kingdom of God
The Story of Scripture

SEEKERS
Encountering Jesus
Jesus the Reason
Meeting Jesus

LEADERS
Christian Leadership
Integrity
Elijah
Joseph

**SHAPING YOUR
CHARACTER**
Christian Character
Decisions
Self-Esteem
Parables
Pleasing God

Woman of God
*Women of the
New Testament*
*Women of the
Old Testament*

**LIVING FULLY
AT EVERY STAGE**
Singleness
Marriage
Parenting
*Couples of the
Old Testament*
*Couples of the
New Testament*
*Growing Older
& Wiser*

**REACHING
OUR WORLD**
Missions
Evangelism
Four Great Loves
Loving Justice

LIVING YOUR FAITH
Busyness
Christian Virtues
Forgiveness

**GROWING IN
RELATIONSHIPS**
Christian Community
Friendship

Find the perfect study for your group with IVP's LifeGuide Finder:
ivpress.com/lifeguidefinder